Borrowed Landscapes

PETER SCUPHAM was born in Liverpool in 1933 and studied at Emmanuel College, Cambridge. He founded the Mandeville Press with John Mole. He was given a Cholmondeley Award in 1996 and is a Fellow of the Royal Society of Literature. Peter Scupham has published a number of poetry collections with Oxford University Press and Anvil. Carcanet publish his *Collected Poems* (2003), and his edition of selections from Arthur Golding's translation of Ovid's *Metamorphoses* (2005). He lives in Norfolk where he runs an antiquarian book business with Margaret Steward.

T0164295

PETER SCUPHAM

Borrowed Landscapes

CARCANET

Acknowledgements

Some of these poems have appeared in *The Rialto*, *PN Review*, *OxfordPoets 2001*, A Treasury of Love Poems (Book Blocks), Christmas Books (Mandeville Press), and the *Emmanuel College Magazine*. 'Out of Season' was published in a limited edition by the Chestnut Press. 'Seventy Years a Showman' was shortlisted for the Forward Prize for Best Single Poem, 2006, and appeared in *The Forward Book of Poetry*, 2006.

First published in Great Britain in 2011 by
Carcanet Press Limited
Alliance House
Cross Street
Manchester M2 7AQ

A CIP catalogue record for this book is available from the British Library

ISBN 978 1 84777 080 6

The publisher acknowledges financial assistance from Arts Council England

Supported by
ARTS COUNCIL
ENGLAND

Typeset by XL Publishing Services, Tiverton
Printed and bound in England by SRP Ltd, Exeter

Contents

The Old Type Tray

for Roger Burford Mason, 1943-1998

Here triune orchid, Caesar, swan,
find Auden's common box, lie down
in beds of loose and lettered gravel;
patience now must undishevel
    feathers, tongues and petals long dispelled –
    the case is everything which is the world.

Collected Works, Principia,
primal scream and earliest ur,
tall talk, the latest from the street
where Caliban, Miranda meet
    spill from this crazy leaden casket, still
    packed to the brim with hope and syllable.

For words – which grew from thinginess –
have cast their spells in metal dress,
each petalled, feather-light impression
a stay against their distribution:
    typographer and text, the clock defied,
    put to their final proof and justified.

Figures in a Landscape, 1944

for John and Mary Mole

*We could hear the oncoming doodle-bug behind us chugging like a motor bike,
in front of us on a rise to the left we saw two semi-detached houses. A man was
digging in a garden alongside, a little boy was running up the garden path
towards the house... at the doorway was a woman beckoning him to hurry
indoors... there was a loud explosion, a mushroom cloud of dust. Everything
went up; no houses, no man, no mother and no boy. We picked up three dust-
bins full of pieces out of the rubble. The only way to identify where they were
was the dampening dust and the cloud of flies.*
Stanley Rothwell, Lambeth at War (SE1 People's History
Project, 1981), *quoted by Jane Stevenson in* Edward Burra:
A Twentieth Century Eye *(Jonathan Cape, 2007)*

I

How busy, busy, busy these ghosts are,
who pack away their bones and wrinkles,
roll ashen sleeves up for the duration.

She ties time back to its apron strings,
puts up her hair in a nest of curlers.
They cling tight for a safe rough-ride

when she pummels and scrubs life stupid,
sets the Vactric moaning like a siren,
pegs out her tempers to the washing-line.

He buffs up his blue, chalk-striped trousers,
snaps the jaws of his briefcase shut
on dull certificates of proficiency,

sets out in khaki on a croaking push-bike
for sticky-bombs, firecrackers, clay grenades,
the Captain's chalk-and-talk in the Village Hall.

Their children's job is just to shrink a little,
cut rinds of mud from square-toed shoes,
trundle dolly about in a deadbeat pram

while the wireless wraps house and garden
in creamy sheets of taratantara.
Housewives without choice, workers without playtime

work themselves back again to skim and bone.
The dustmen make *schräge musik* with the bins,
swinging us all to the grave on stooped shoulders.

II

Big flowers lean to the sun,
blonde village simpletons,
dirt faces picked to moons

like the one I watch climb,
pause out on a limb
of a tree I can't name

in a place I called home.
Each dissolving room
rubs to the same

patch of distempered wall
made gestural
by Van Gogh's chorale:

sunflowers with yellow heads
A Zouave's brilliant red,
a blue cart in a field

their licks of paint all
primary, primal.
The world before this fall

into unlit green and brown
where the big flowers lean
and bombers groan.

III

In a flat-faced semi on the road out
shaky taps have left their misery running.
Garden-skins souse in slurps of cess
or loll and sunburn to a sour frizz.
Is it Charlie Holmes, digging in his patch,
in battledress, in summer, in silence?
At the window I watch our neighbour's child
go riding down the gravel in his coffin,

watch Charlie, Father: patched and taciturn
as guys or scarecrows, whose hands
cradle potatoes like misshapen eggs
wring chickens' necks, drown kittens.
Houses brim with slow, hoarded anger;
spill to outbursts of wild sobbing.
Mens' work is burial, exhumation;
the clay weeps at their slicing spades.

IV

War, cat-like, hoards nine lives
in dust-scribbles, boxes of dull silence.
Here the boy cupboards his ruinous loves –
bomb-fins, tracer-shells and shrapnel –
hunkers them down with the cold pond-life
of eggs in isinglass, window-panes
furred white with webbing, trunks of trunks
stretched out headless on a cage of rafters.

My rod propped against the garage door,
I turn, paw the shelf to find my gentles:
glistening maggots packed like shelter-sleepers.
Fingers tingle on a fizzing tin
of flesh-flies greedy for the hidden light.
Wings and legs tangle into vortex –
unscrew away from their dispersal point,
sing a dark song back into its ghost.

V

Pain is so far away it has become lyrical,
its edge keening in a dramatic present
where the world dances to sweet, high music:
plucked wire, hen squawks, a child screaming,
the grasshopper tick of a bike wheel spun free
between its tuning forks. Down the school road
small village sirens and their bully boys
sing their piss into buckets of warm straw.

Bass-notes: the labouring gear-change of a truck,
slap of wet sheets in a drying wind,
silver bombers wrapped in quiet thunder
floating east over westering buzz-bombs:
feral waifs combing the low highways.
She stands alert, carved out of stony time
in a cold kitchen, in a cold house,
a silence neither of us has the heart to break.

VI

Criss-cross, mud-shod,
he scrambles the ditch-lines,
notches pithed elder
to whistle up a wind

to blow them all away:
con-trails, cobwebs,
sobbing, anger,
the blue smoke-tang

hovering a penny
perched on the line:
a king's face blurred
by the hammering wheels.

Down wind, wires thrum;
a pole's china insulator
falls to his catapult's
four-square elastic.

Never such innocence
on his round cat-face,
purring up the drive,
a bomb in his basket,

Like other boys
who go out, early,
come back, late,
do nothing, much,

but race down paths
where mothers beckon
and men in braces
turn things over.

VII

Beggar my neighbour and take the rap.
From *Mondscheinsonate* to *Thunderclap*,
Coventry, Freiburg sear the map.

Do the little dogs laugh to see such fun?
How can the dish run away with the spoon
when moon refuses to rhyme with June,

and anything, everything, anything goes,
the umbrellas to mend, the holes in their clothes,
the rings on their fingers, the bells on their toes,

the jug with no handle, the half-burnt candle,
Monday's washing done up in a bundle,
the Bible, Shakespeare, Brahms and Handel.

'Lie in the dark and listen.' I do,
and hear the shake of them passing through
as each earnest, chaffering, murderous crew

of the Sorcerers' clever apprentices
blows by sky-high to turn is to was
and only a pen to turn was to is.

No Odes to Nightingales, or Joy,
but built from the plainest light of day,
houses: a man, a mother, a boy

who dance in the dark with clapped-out eyes
through blood and treasure, is, will be, was,
through dampening dust and a cloud of flies.

The Way

Only known like the back of a hand –
running fissure, old scar tissue
dull as milkskin –

where finger-posts lie down in shadow
and from miles on miles of sad
fantastic voices

pencil in each indirection
to soft as cat fur, hard as pack drill,
blue as distance.

There crooked men run crooked miles
over crunched and stumbled hills.
Proud flesh festers.

Never known like the front of a hand,
plump with furious, destined roads,
cross and crescent,

where the pack of pretty straight guys
limp in shoes packed stone-tight
to the deadest ends,

bend the right map to the wrong crease,
rim a hill's white knucklebone
on the one contour,

plagued by backhand sounds of children
filling alley, track and backstreet
with laughter, sobbing…

Estuary

Myriads of stones knock their heads together.
chatterboxing under that mew, mew, mew.
Come clean to this confluence of waters;
turn your back on the loneliness of windows
and, sick as Lazarus with his single death,
feel for life, the hauling in, the ebb of it

where slips of tide follow their own creases
this way, that way, by a crooked gantry
signifying loss, which has its own nine bouges,
its own bedevillings. These wraiths of sea-mist
nibble the heart out, have a cunning
to sting your fingers to crossed purposes,

reveal no more than shallow stains of lichen
hooped by rust, your softened footprints.
As marram grass keens about this Golgotha,
let the spilt brains of weed and bladderwrack
show you the separations of the self
and the frost wind take your bearings

off out to sea, beating an iron drum
of half-sunk cogs which snap at nothing.
Pay out and further out your lines of thought,
hear wind and water sing – if you can bear the burden
which thrills through blocks and baulks and wires
littered on the shiftless, shifting sand –

of how the sea bobs with familiar faces:
the dead you rescued and the dead you drowned,
how, to the landward of your field of vision,
breed further fluctuations of the hour:
the outstretched hands you long ago let slip,
the loving voices which would call you home.

Out of Season

Gulls haul the night wind in and over it all,
squabble for chit-chat spilling from lip and bin:
crumbs of comfort grown ever more comfortless
soused in this mizzle which eases against the grain.

Patches of light die out from the east, and pause
over little glisters of pain which nest in leaves;
curtains are drawn, thin films of mucus trail
where snailshells close upon our sucked-in loves.

Out there, ever and all ways, fathoms of time
and a blackening sky rock water and inshore wind;
floats bob-bob about at the ends of their tethers,
a long, deep sigh heaves out to the town beyond

where the old move dully about in their dated plumage,
talk in low cries of the ghosts they have become.
Their eyes in their drying rings pull for the light;
at the turn of the tide each faces the climb for home,

the drag of a shadow-self to the kitchen door
where the fuchsia dims down its lantern-lights of blood
and the gulls wheel with the furies over the roof,
mewing in animal grief for the quick and the dead.

The Singing Field

for Nigel Forde

Something is out of breath and singing of home
in a stadium filled with invisible come-and-go:
that sea-sift sigh which falls on children's ears
who sail their beds in a darkened bungalow,
cross, re-cross the shoals of awake and asleep.

Tuned to this field, brimmed with my blood, a shell
for listening-in which is neither here nor there,
I move to a static hiss, the tune of a de-icing fridge
whose magnetic words: *cavern, sublime, despair,*
offer lorelei visions of mountain and castle-keep,

then shake my head away from such siren tinnitus,
this hushing of tumbling hair teased by the comb,
these urgent sibilant whispers of long-dead girls,
telling over and over their *mémoires d'outre-tombe,*
in a quickening chafe and rasp of dry on dry.

The stopped clouds are clean out of breath; the sun
is a furnace fuelled by stammering ciphers of sound.
Earth-creatures sing as they rise to the shock of light,
new life struck from darkly encumbered ground.
The dead croon softly, moonily, where they lie.

Out There

About the stiffish fields, the rooks
       tear pieces from the sky,
rats and mice and such small deer
cling to the turning of the year –
       crisp claw and wary eye.

The sobbing daylight makes a space
       for legend and for loss
by creak and crevice, stings of rain,
by faces melting on the pane,
       the tall trees' pitch and toss.

The stars are blowing into snow,
       the snow blows into stars –
old Peg-leg in his lantern coat,
a skein of silk flown from his throat,
       glints through your glazing-bars,

and Broomsticks, to the rising moon,
       goes creeping after kind –
Draw close the curtain, light the fire
against this feral, chill desire
       that rides upon the wind.

Three Evening Pastorals

Scarecrows

Zig-zags of migraine
ribbon the wind's tail.
They're at it again,
sprinkling ghost-seed:
a wardrobe scraped,
a drawing-book plundered

for peg-legs, face-cloths.
Hands in spasm
surrender a greeting,
the once-bold tenantry
of farmer, squarson,
take the field,

slack heads crowned
with cast-off thinking caps.
Ill-tricked, ill-treated
by this eviction,
no soft candles
glow in their brain-pans

and no news now
from the long western front.
Sun goes down
letting them dangle –
moon's kissing cousins.
Clouds haul black

over wool-gathering
nail and thorn,
nightmares hung
on the old barbed wire.
Monstrous crows
quarrel over eyes.

It

It's hung about like this
since someone left it in the rain.
When it ran out of puff or juice,
there was, it seems,
no need to haul the bugger back again.

Ridiculous to say
that someone left it in the *sun*,
hunkered for nettles, grass waist-high,
perched awkwardly
on bits and bobs which slowly came undone

and came undone, till rust
locked joint and jaw, made a one thing
of countless disparate motions lost
in a blue mist,
exhausted fumes, another evening.

A spit-and-polish love
once called it by its proper name
then swore at it. Dead and alive,
as weathers give
their air of difference to what stays the same

it begs the passing days
with tales of love locked out, the slide
to unaccommodation, all those
necessities
so fiercely asked by us, and then denied.

Set-aside

The day makes dull report.
Scared birds twist
in failing wind;
high cirrus floated on light,
teases to side-slip.

Heavy metal
ploughs field-names under.
On the headland
ivied oaks patrol
the night's enclosures;

stump hedges
thrashed into obedience
mark out lost pounds
to keep the cash
from straying,

and cropped pages dull
both text and gloss
to the *decent obscurity*
of a language
dead to our horizons.

A tawny moon
deepens to eclipse;
the fields blacken
into charred setaside,
and Orion stumbles.

As the cusp comes clean
two owls rehearse
a little oral history
from choirs of cooling air
and places where they sing.

A Civil War

for Roger Scupham

In the 1880s two related academic German families were invited to take up positions in Cambridge: the Braunholtzes and the Breuls. Eugen Braunholtz, Fellow of King's, Reader in Romance Languages, had four sons, who were educated in British public schools and served with the British forces in the Great War. Hermann Braunholtz, my father-in-law, later Keeper of the Ethnographical Collections at the British Museum, served in the ranks of the R.A.M.C. on the Western Front. This sequence, drawing on family records and his diaries, was occasioned by the meeting of two combatant survivors, Henry Allingham and Robert Meier, at Wetten, Germany, in November, 2006.

Wildstrubel, 1913

He watched two Germans gather alpenrosen, singing,
as a shaft of sunlight travelled from forest to snow.
Clouded avalanches shook the slopes above him.

Saw further snows that 'rode across the sky
like surf grizzling the rock-entangled sea,
the turbid river, snow-born, nourished by the sun'.

Climbed piled zig-zags to the Wildstrubel Hotel:
pretty done in, managed to fight his way
through a verandah packed with cheering schoolgirls.

Picked roses, left them behind, went on
down very bewildering paths in villages,
past quaint houses, 'children peeping out at odd corners',

Left the Valais Alps 'entangled largely in cloud',
was cheered by a boy yodelling far below him.
Later, in a wood, drank dew from leaves.

Such enormous trifles chequering the world
must not be forgotten: must be forgotten.
Their invisible load is too much for us to carry.

Shall I send them all into the deepening dark:
the youthful singers, the laughing girls, the boy,
those inquisitive children at their wooden doorways,

and two Englishmen in puttees, green town-coats,
clutching Cook's tourist tickets, a lad with his mule,
a 'uniformed humbug' at the Douane in Calais?

You tiny wraiths of long-gone summer days
as bright and small as insect-life in grass,
be busy still about your pleasures, duties.

Christmas: Hanover, France, Cambridge, 1914

'Then my Christmas letter, intended for you all,
gathered together at home in England
did not arrive in time – perhaps it never came?
So much, now, we cannot freely talk about
that we should keenly wish to thresh out openly.
Your letter, though, was a special pleasure to me,
expressing that fundamental idea,
the one so important to each one of us:
we shall, and will, in unchanged heartiness,
preserve our personal relationships,
especially so within the family circle.
This is a matter which closely touches the heart.'

Merry Christmas! Fröhliche Weihnachten!

Time now, at the concertina's lilt and squeeze,
to raise chalked boards above the parapet,
a candled tree, a song, a lucky head.

Throw off pouch and rifle, clamber out,
laugh and jest under drifting cigarette smoke,
(Webley and Luger bedded in their holsters),
close the early dead in their first graves.

Exchange buttons, booze and badges,
drink a toast to 'Wives and Sweethearts',
play kickabout in No Man's Land,

'Cousin, it is little use talking now.
I do not want to see either side suffer badly,
though I fear both are going to do so.
The Anthropological Institute has decided
to elect no honorary fellows this year.
As our President said at the last Council Meeting,
it would be unfair to omit distinguished Germans,
and we must never confuse science with politics.

My personal feelings to my relations and friends are quite unchanged. I love Germany, I feel for it, but I am not sure whether cousin Otto was not right to give his services to this, our country.'

Adams Road, 1915

Poor father and mother. Their position must be very hard, as, of course, their sympathies are strong on both sides; and so are mine. And if I fought against my own relations and the people to whom, by blood, I belong, and am proud to belong, it would not be out of my wish to injure them, but only because I consider my duty is clearly to this my country.

In Cambridge, the leaves are dry and loquacious
and the light is accustomed to propositions
which the wind, travelling from corner to corner,
confutes in a flurry of grey cloudscapes.

King's Chapel, Lawrence's 'sow with piglets',
bruises her teats on the cold, enlightened air;
the walrus dons, their apron-strings unloosed,
mourn in their cups for pretty officers.

At 'Goslar', Adams Road, exact scholarship
dusts the still rooms. Elisabeth, in her German Garden,
prunes roses as Eugen prunes his language-thickets.
All is echt Deutsch. Keats is an anagram of Skeat.

The philologist and his wife have four fine sons:
by England, out of Prussia. Off to lose their fortunes,
the lucks of their civil war to end war will be kind
to Gustav, Hermann, Eugen, young Walter,

who all turn obediently into sepia, the colour
much favoured by that cusp of time where history
drags at memory, its fearsome hunger
digesting our conversations into static.

The shadows on this photograph lie very steadily,
and the young men have left the playing field
to an old horse harnessed to the heavy roller;
it pauses briefly and forever at its flattening task.

42nd Motorised Ambulance Company, 1916–1918

I am in a school where book-knowledge, previously acquired learning, as such, counts for nothing. Knowledge of character, handling men, action, are everything. I might as well have omitted all my school and academic career. I am also cut off by an almost impenetrable barrier from all those young officers with whom I am by birth and education naturally inclined to associate. It is an excellent tonic for the germ of vanity and snobbishness.

With common nouns, proper to the occasion,
call the roster of a peace-time wardrobe –
winter suits: one brown (old),
purple woollen waistcoat to match:
one grey-black, two trousers,
blue-spotted waistcoat to match:
one blue-black, two trousers:
one grey tweed suit ('Norway')
with knickers. Close the door on it all:
white flannels, Aertex, rain and overcoats,
their sober-sided cloth-and-cotton-talk
of bats, balls, skates and alpenstocks.

Now, proper names, common as dirt and blood,
unravel and confirm new litanies,
appropriate to the matter, and the service:
Epernay, Courcemain, Montmirail,
Abbeville, Beaumont are cross-threaded
by fifty Talbot ambulances,
two Vauxhall staff-cars,
four Thorneycroft lorries
and seven Triumph motorbikes.
'Shut up', 'Switch off', 'Park up'.
They cool safely, shadowed by his diary,

and muster, in their khaki dressing
with Captain Pearmain ('Spearmint'),
'Darky' Robinson (Bronco Bill's Circus),
'Bon-bon' Ashford, Lieutenant Galpin,
'Titch' Pope (batman, general buffoon),
'Bruiser' Edmonds and Whitelock (burglar).

Also two Germans, 'Bosch' and 'Fritz',
met on a piano-hunt in Escandoeures,
still jesting about their latest escapade
gnawed by rats, one with his skull blown off.
Words dry-clean their field-grey shroudings.

'Heavy shelling – cover ambulance roofs with branches;
order countermanded as contrary to Red Cross rules –
gas shells coming over – two drowned by shell in river –
hear 'La Grosse Bertha' – bathe in wood in tin tub –
breakdowns – tyres melting – buy whiskey for O.C.
   Shelling now intermittent.

Lose Talbot driver – car smashed – O.C. laconic –
rumour of move to Italy – Jerry advances across Marne;
builds fourteen new bridges – pushed back today.
'Jocks' take heavy casualties – letters from home –
accompany wounded to Sézanne – petrol dump on fire.
   Severe cases. Rough roads.

To Vertus with Cox – Cox's remarkable behaviour –
new offensive on Amiens front – all cars away –
four Military Medals awarded for Epernay push –
"Jerry" over flying low – our shrapnel just missed me –
Aubigny – pick up man shot in stomach, dying.
   Read *Henry Rycroft*.

Admonished for hanging blankets on a garden fence –
out with car on Arras-Cambrai road – Hindenburg line –
dugout a hundred steps down – dead machine-gunners;
lunch there – see Vimy Ridge, observation balloons –
light raid at night – four bombs fall near canteen.
   Terrific thunderstorm.

ARMISTICE signed at 5.00 a.m. – takes effect at 11.00 –
Bavaria declares a Republic – revolution in Berlin –
Kings of Bavaria, Hesse, Saxony etc. dethroned or in flight –
Valenciennes: Hôtel de Ville decorated – no demonstrations –
climbed tower of church – the frenzied sexton,
   a Tommy ringing the bell!'

He talks with scholars and the rational dead:
Huxley, Tylor, Fraser. A hunter-gatherer,
he reassembles Stone Age Africa in London,
conjuring the basements into armouries
where night and silence hoard unshaken spears.

Quotations, admirations and memoranda
jostle for space in each *Museum Overland Tablet.*
Reading Stevenson, he finds a companion, loves
'the generous humanity that shines all through his work'.
In committee he scribbles light verse for colleagues,

revisits his notes on the late tribal wars,
inking over his pencilled glimmerings:
A dago is anyone what isn't our sort of chap,
For there's no life, when it's war to the knife,
Like the life of the R.A.M.C. Forbidden to put Dirt.

His brother Eugen, kindly and bespectacled,
a medical orderly on the Somme, at Passchendaele,
teaches at Wellington, lives quietly with his cat.
They converse in the dialect of their tribe,
share walks and head-colds in a salvo of postcards.

In his forties, he marries a quiet girl from Somerville
who pastes default labels on surgical bric-a-brac
for Henry Wellcome: *Curious Object, Use Unknown;*
her brother, a Captain in the Royal Welch,
dies in action on the retreat to Dunkirk.

As it all begins again, he packs up the Collections
for Quex Park and its wildlife skins and bones:
(Oubangai: Major Powell-Cotton in the field,
photographed as if in his natural habitat:
note the tin of Glaxo baby-powder, the fertility doll).

Here, all ranks mounted equally by Rowland Ward,
stuffed and nonsense glare from dioramas.
Records show where each specimen was shot,
which might also, with tolerable accuracy
be deduced from headstones, records of courts martial.

He watches London burn from the Museum roof.
When Lancasters breach the Möhne and Eder dams
his people hang from drowned trees down the Ruhr;
when Donner and Blitzen set the fire-bells jingling
he shares his Christmas Day with German prisoners.

Torre House, Harpenden, 1963

He and the quiet rooms consider their dying,
Time hangs about. It has nowhere else to go,
nothing much to do. Toepffer: *Garde tes songes,*
les sages n'en ont pas aussi beaux que les sots.
It is down in indelible pencil. He and the house
dream thing to image, image again to thing
in this place for everything, with nothing in place.
Cousin Hanne comes to help nurse his passing.

Humped asleep in the shabby conservatory,
congealed and yellowing bundles of *The Times*
give column inches to the obituaries
of flies and spiders morgue-filed wing to limb.
Runes inscribe his darkness: letters from France,
a card: *Place Safe. Doctors Visit*, a winding trail
of movement-orders, billets, chits for 'essence',
Lieutenant Galpin's parting gift – his Juvenal.

Black Chimu birds that you can whistle through
sit cheek by jowl with papier-mâché brutes
from funerary Mexico. Peru, teroo,
they softly call. Dalmatian double-flutes
rise to a hiss of air, the propellor's buzz
as he joy-rides a yellow Spad through Picard sky,
goggled, strapped to the 'quiver, the motionless poise
which irresistibly suggests a dragonfly'.

The emeritus Keeper of Ethnography
knows nothing is lost and nothing can be found.
He is the dream crazing the cluttered study
where I formally asked him for his daughter's hand,
looting cherries, watching 'Jerry' downed in flame,
soldier, scholar-gypsy. In his dead, slow-dying war,
he calls on Dr Hublard, Conservator, who tells him:
Vous serez toujours le bienvenu, Monsieur,

He feels roses entwine him, skates on the flooded fens
as cloths and rugs mourn over the cluttered floor;
carbon-datings of pots, flints, scratch-nib pens,
place the garage-bills at nineteen twenty-four.
His last post caught, the piano plays Brahms to itself,
pine-shadowed snows wave goodbye from the wall;
his received pronunciation lies taped on the shelf,
the convoy proceeds to Stopsley (Ave atque) Vale.

Wetten, November 2006

The oldest veterans of the Great War met in Wetten, Germany, and placed a wreath on the war memorial. Their combined age was 219. They hugged, shook hands: 'It's wonderful to be together. Everyone has to be friends.'

Henry Allingham, Robert Meier,
step forward with the dead;
they move, enchanted, through their war,
strip-searched by flame and flood.
How should they know that each was born
to be the other's good?

The latest living eyes and hands
of that stupendous host,
each, at the century's command,
patrols the other's ghost,
the heavy stations of their cross
their observation post.

Henry Allingham, Robert Meier,
step forward with the dead.
They move as wreath and stone require.
Embrace. Rain, wind and cloud
re-muster ranked and numbered names
known only unto God.

The Hunt

The Gallery, Old Hall, South Burlingham

I

The hunt will soon be up.
Morning trips and jingles
to walls whose bright lime
sharpens the scent,
prepares the ground.

Wands of ochre, charcoal,
conjure for stag and boar
a pack, a harbourer.
Close doublets of leaves
are slashed on light

sprawled between fingers,
bracken, spear-grass.
Grisaille weaves a net,
winding the mort
for this pinched Meet

with coal-black eyes
who must quarry out
four centuries
of spellbound sunlight.
Where collared oak

springs from tie-beams,
dry reeds whisper
their long recheat:
the far tristesse
of Plenty's horn.

II

Lymier, limier, can de traella,
your quest the solitary heart
foliaged in guile and innocence,

work to the high recess of summer
through passages of sun and silence,
alert for one small token

to ease the unslaked mouth,
that sadness hung about the eyes,
these curtains of white darkness.

III

For sadness, too, writes white.
Skin upon skin of lime –
nine skins to the long unmaking
for hunters lost in the snow.
Hammocks of dirt and frost

rock the trees to sleep
in cold Broceliande.
The room is a dark lantern
and something bays at the moon;
cloud, star and hour

slip westward nightly,
dust the window-square.
Over-wintering peacocks
wake up to die
as glass claps at their wings.

And these, too, ache for light,
poor disjecta membra:
untoothed saws of bracken
a boar's raised fell,
the fury of small eyes.

Skin upon skin of sky
settles vaguely on this.
A hunter parts his curtain,
swings a half-sword
at nothing, afraid and crouching.

Shredded with Rose

In a room shredded with melancholy rose,
a few scraped arabesques, a treillage,
diaperings of charcoal – pretty patch-words –
the wide oak floorboards furred with silver
and tanged by thorns of brittle iron
step to once-a-door: a half-discovery,
a stopped sentence. Consider how
a child hunts the maze its fingers make,
pausing in rounds and lozenges of nowhere
to set a wrong course for its own deep centre,
that garden-centre urn on a coarse pedestal
fills with yesterday and dust, the Minotaur
paws with chipped hooves in sullen patience.
At this, your frontier and your point of entry,
a slip might change your vista into visa,

admit a journey through a carious landscape
alive with one-armed bandits, limbo-dancers,
travellers in dust and suchlike furnishings.
Short work to knock, be greeted by a hole
down which that sweet and lovely populace
could slip into the thinnest of thin airs.
Imagine a door: the slats, the Suffolk latch
as plausible as a long dash and comma.
Its boards, licked white, play open, shut,
disturb the light. Take space in your stride.
convince yourself you are a heartbeat nearer
that thing which cries with all its weight of being
'Love me. I am your crying need, the one,
the needle's eye, the burnt fire in the clearing' –
and face, snow-blind, the wall's fresh assertion..

Generations

Drawn down, deep down,
by the ebbing year,
butterflies quiver
in clapped-out shawls,
rain rubs clean
scrapped mice on stones.

We watch our house-carls:
a tumbling cat
in a snuff-spot suit;
his playboy confrère,
a toe-tip dancer
trimmed in thistledown.

For blood and scamper
they whet slit eyes
on dumbed-down light;
against the cold
we wrap ourselves
in their generations.

Spots

This bovine cat has garden light in his eyes,
tobacco-stained fur, a smell of drying hay.
As we butt our lazy heads in a Glasgow kiss
he flicks his notched and see-through ears,
their skins worn down to a stiff oilcloth. Then,
a clumsy thump and sprawl on my scribbled page

where words hunt in packs, teasing a memory,
out of a date, a time: the eleventh hour
on the warm sixteenth of a cool September.
They tell you how cool air leafs through his hairs,
how cusps of lemon-yellow crooked for the light
dangle among the honeysuckle's blazing berries

and lose their threads in a singleness of green
where every shadow clings to intricate substance,
and every substance falls into simple shadow.
He snaps away at his tail, shudders his head,
sticks a leg over a shoulder to lick his arse –
ridiculous as a ham frilled in a cookery book –

and pinpoints a tortoiseshell spreading its petals
on the stem of something simple I cannot name,
this late summer sun gilding his autumn coat.
When I fondle his throbbing chest, its motors idling
with sounds that only my fingertips can hear,
he sings of the garden and love like an old brown shell.

Goodman

A cat for all seasons – don't you know
this particular one-cat, cat to go,
black-and-white mousing-minstrel show?

A tom by birth, but a bit of fluff:
plumpish, plush, a powder-puff
with a hanging judge's cap, a buff

smudge on a snub nose,
pink pads and a dancer's toes,
he shall have music wherever he goes.

A smallish cat with a largeish purr,
gooseberry eyes, angora fur,
agog for whiskabout and stir

as he beats his bounds, out on a roll
for the garden rabbit-and-hen patrol,
then top-up fish in his begging bowl.

A kitchen side-step, slither and glide,
a call to arms for an upstairs ride –
he's well in touch with his feminine side,

this odalisque, all sprawl and spread,
with wrap-round paws for your wrist in bed,
a dumb-struck, wide-eyed sleepyhead.

Cat and Mouse

It's a cat-and-mouse performance,
twitching at the curtain
for stuff that isn't there,
trying to catch the voices,
loving, lost, uncertain,
trembled into air.

Though the light is steady
from the yellow candle-flames
tiptoed on the tree,
all the snows we ever knew
are whirling out of yesterday
to bury you and me.

There! Pull it out of hiding!
As fast as we unwrap it
it slips into ago –
and yet – my clumsy fingers
trip on kisses falling
through the falling snow.

A Merry-go-round for Megan

If you start from *here*,
you could end up *there*,
on a roundabout
with a dragon and a star
and a wide-eyed owl
and a three-wheeled car,
always in the middle
wherever you may be,
the riddle in the middle
of the place called ME.

Reindeer, rabbits, roses,
necklaces and noses,
crawly-creeps and bouncers,
paddy-paws and pouncers.
shut-me-ups and talkers,
whiskalongs and walkers,
watch the birds, watch the snow,
watch the people come and go
fast, slow – but you know

if you start from *there*,
you could end up *here*,
with a mouse and a cat
and a fancy that,
with a dog and a frog
and a velvet hat,
always in the middle
wherever you may be,
the riddle in the middle
of the place called ME!

May

for Margaret

I watch you smile for these pale fable-bearers
who brighten in the passing wake of shadow
pitched by a sun which sets the garden flying.
Their proper, common names, shrouded in green,
lie quiet as black loam, as alluvial pebbles
dull with earth-glow, as husky stems that die back
into a stump-work of clay and cobbles.

Today, the calendar brings round your name-day,
the year pares to the quick – Mais, Magius,
whose root signifies new growth, sap rising:
the copse hemmed in, stitched-up by Queen Anne's Lace,
Cow Parsley, Gipsy's Curtain, Lady's Needlework.
Our late paths close to one dark runnelling
through the rough, heady scent, as moonlight

bares this, the frailest of those English ghosts,
whose long processional canopies nod by
hooding their soldier-beetles, forkytails:
Hedge Parsley, Hemlock, Hogweed, Alexander,
all keep their simple virtues, reach for light
with a green darkness piping through their stems:
Puck's Needle, Devil's Nightcap, Bad Man's Oatmeal,

and, stronger for culling on the orchard floor,
not yet Dog Daisy of the long dog days –
the Moon's Eye, Mowing Daisy of high summer –
but Bellis Perennis, La Belle Marguerite,
The Pearl, the Eye of Day, her white-and-red
wearing your name, the shadow of your substance,
the substance of your shadow: mortal flesh.

Borrowed Landscapes

Shall we raise up the dead to fringe our garden
and set the wind siffling among their shrouds,
offer the sunset and the quilted clouds
the frissons of a 'Look, no hands!', a dare,
a stroll through chill and rotten-clothy air
past stuff best hidden,

or dress our boundaries with a kinder fiction,
the paper-cut of a remembered hill;
watch a smooth sheen of ancient light infill
a ruined cloister, paint a woodland gold,
let some pavilion hide in pleat and fold
its cold attraction?

Such borrowings of no and yes embellish
the average of our moulting hens, our gnomes
gone fishing, the un-mobile homes
flat-tyred in nettles, the quotidian tracts
of washings-up and matterings of facts,
all spit, no polish,

but when the night-shift wheels on scenery
to prop against our loves, our hopes, our dread;
strange locomotions twist and twirl the bed
through landscapes taut with absence, vertigo,
devised by Piranesi, Chirico –
chicanes, chicanery,

and stuff reforms in close, tumultuous air:
a spouting whale swims through a college court,
Beau Geste props up a corpse to man a fort
beaten to flowers sixty years ago,
patched children dance with soldiers in the snow
and 'Who goes there?'

throbs a tin sentry, helmeted in shade
from the high window of the Bridge Café.
The flag-day floats go puddering on their way,
collection boxes rattle, faces lift
their molten features to the sun, then shift
this promenade

to some place at the back of God knows where
leaving us image-naked, and alone
with cryptogenic thoughts as dry as bone,
with night and day, which beat us black and blue,
with unstocked fields, and two crows for a view –
all bare, bare, bare –

but where's the landscape that we didn't borrow?
Each ring-fenced hortus where we make our stand
betrays our footprints to its shifting sand,
confiding every secret smile or sigh
to the closed circuit of a landscaped eye
focused on zero

or tail-lights on some travelling circus, where
zanies, apes, acrobats with spangled tabards
and smiling girls who wait in icy cupboards
for Mr Right and his bunch of skeleton keys
twist your own echo back upon the breeze
Ah, were you there!

Seventy Years a Showman

'Lord' George Sanger grows up

1833, Oxford. Hilton's drivers try to pass Wombwell's:
a clash of crowbars, tent-poles, whips. *The fat man*
made for the living skeleton with a door hook;
the skeleton batters the fat man with a peg mallet.
Wombwell's elephants break their wagon to splinters
while *two little trembling figures, in our night-gowns*,
press at their caravan windows. It goes down blazing.

At six years old, he works the family peepshow,
a mite *in a clean pinafore and well-greased boots*
pattering the death of Maria Marten by William Corder
in the famous Red Barn. At twenty-six peepholes
strings tighten on Corder's neck by tallow candlelight;
at the Red Lion, Wantage, a wretch with a fagging-hook
half-severs the landlady's head. *All was confusion.*

Learn the moral. *Keep your temper, my boys,*
keep your temper. The peepshow is briskly altered:
a cut-up woman, taproom, savage sickleman – *and with*
a plentiful supply of carmine for gore, the trick was done.
Newbury is all smallpox, bells and funerals. Father
braces each child's arm with a darning-needle, rubs in
pustular serum. *The results were all that could be wished,*

and winter-work is carrying goods round Berkshire.
At the Bell and Bottle two strangers beg a lift, hoist
a parcel of duds and things for a little job on the back rail.
He loosens the sack, and glimpses, bared by moonlight,
the pallid, wax-like face of a dead woman. Trembling,
he gives way, drops off the wagon, runs to catch it up –
Georgie, not a word! Keep on by the side of the horses!

Watching his passengers drowse off, Father pulls up
by a fellow wagoner whose boy races for assistance,
then cracks on into a mob *armed with pitchforks, cudgels,*
and other rustic weapons who haul away the bodysnatchers.
Next summer, Father's blunderbuss guards the caravan
while thirty thousand Chartists tramp by to sack Newport.
When twenty-four soldiers drop the leaders by musket-fire

'The Riots at Newport' quickly revamps the peepshow,
but at Lansdown Fair Bath roughs led by Carroty Kate –
strong as a navvy, a big brutal animal – wreck the booths
in a frenzy of drink, fire and mayhem. The showmen
yoke the wreckers on tent-ropes, drag them through water,
trice them to wheels, thrash them with whalebone whips:
Three dozen for every man jack of 'em. Lay on, boys!

On Romney Marsh, he slips on a roundabout. A *bolt*
literally tore the flesh of the calf away from the limb.
Father, who fought with Nelson on the Victory,
saddles up the horse, rides three miles for a doctor,
refuses amputation, sews back the calf, sailor-fashion –
sixteen huge stitches looping the silk. *Don't halloa,*
it'll soon be finished! Be a man, Georgie!

Glad when Nellie gives up *the Lion Queen business*,
he's off to Stalybridge Wakes, where a row breaks out
at the gingerbread stall. Sheppard is kicked to pulp:
a *ghastly shapeless thing in the clear sunlight*,
purple stains blotching the white road-dust.
(Lancashire fights with teeth and iron-tipped clogs.)
That same night the family hears of Father's death,

and in the fall of the year he marries his Nellie.
Life is good with the *Wonderful Performing Fish*,
the *Tame Oyster* and the *Suspension by Ether*.
He performs in a charnel house, buys Astley's,
receives a gold medal from the Ostend Burgomaster,
tricks the Prince of Wales with a whitewashed elephant –
and is murdered in nineteen-eleven by a berserk servant.

At the Window

And, if I ventured out,
where could I hope to go?
Should I search the near and far
through miles of shivering snow
for a burning babe, a star,
or make my peace with my doubt
where waste and wildwood grow?

Safe between these four walls,
the sill cool to my hand,
I watch the garden dressed
by slow, cascading snow,
layer on layer pressed
on those half-remembered falls
where, in the remembered land

I stood at the pane, a child
half-blind in a dazzle of white,
as roof, road, lawn and leaf
confirmed with their robe of snow
my unbelieving belief:
near, far and waste and wild
in the one transforming light.

Flight into Egypt

Some who were warned in dreams to pack and go
across a hasty line ruled in the sand,
found scrub and mirage at the rainbow's end,
the tombs of strangers in occluding snow
and unmade promises in promised land.

Trapped in the cruel nonsenses of things,
they learned their guiding star a marker flare
which drew more darkness down upon their fear;
died by their neighbours' knives, or under blades
whirled into plague about the ice-bound air.

And innocence, which lived a day, then died,
sighs in the ebb-voice of a broken wave
how this one child was cupboarded by love
until his flesh grew ripe, then crucified
by those whose childhood was an open grave.

Unusual Phenomena

See 'Observations upon Unusual Phenomena noted in the Cambridge District, June–August, 1940: The Lethbridge Report, for Mass Observation, from English Anxieties by Tim Brennan (Photoworks, 2009)

The Local Defence Volunteers have been ordered
to note curious signs written on telegraph poles.
Stuck in a cut in the bark of a tree in Harston
was found an advert for Peek Frean's biscuits.
Chalk marks have been seen on adjoining walls.
Agents may be disguised as nuns, or clergymen..

1942. We are welcomed by the Village Idiot
and a man with no roof to the top of his mouth.
I catapult down numerous china insulators
on telegraph poles in Newton Road, Harston,
place a message in a hill-top obelisk
and cunningly make indecipherable chalk marks.

Mutilated cigarette packets have been observed:
Churchman's, Craven A, Black Cat, Weights.
These may well be informative to *the right people*.
There have also been handkerchiefs, bus-tickets…
The English are naturally filthy, but are these really
The *love-signs of a bucolic population*?

My family are disguised as *the wrong people*.
On Saturdays I fetch their packets of Players
from *The Old English Gentleman* at the corner.
They are not love-signs. I use my handkerchiefs
to make parachutes, throw them out of windows,
disguise the stones that weigh them down as nuns.

My father has a Certificate of Proficiency
in the use of the famous *Northover Projector*.
Operated by nuns disguised as clergymen
it fires salvos of Peek Frean's biscuits
at neighbouring obelisks and village idiots.
At the Perse I learn German (not my ticket)

from boards of indecipherable chalk marks.
My friend's dachshund is called Trudi,
but so far we survive, our cover story
not blown away with torn-up leaves from trees
savaged by sheath-knives, heils and achtungs,
cigarette cartons, china insulators.

Who will interpret for us all these cipherings
while the view obtains in our official circles
that these trails now aging, weatherbeaten,
are *Acts of God, maunderings of lovesick yokels*?
One day the truth will out. For now the slogan
Be like Dad, keep Mum, must be my motto.

September Song

Coming in at the front door
with a blue Revelation case
to lug over the mosaic floor
on the first day of an old war –
not a tessera out of place

and every which way to turn,
standing in half-light, mirk
made thicker by so much sun
splashed between now and then.
I can read the dark like a book.

Barrage balloons in place,
tesserae brightening the floor
as a thunderstorm and a war
come in by the swing of a door
on an open and shut case.

She eases the straps to slack.
In the space we anchored down
by lid and sliding lock,
the expanding snore of the rack.
Our shadows kiss and lean

where the mummy-cloths embrace
forgotten, childish gear,
slipping their fast and loose
over dust my crumbling face
spins free to this late, fresh air.

Between the Lines

In a high Victorian house as quiet as reading,
a child stares through a page as white as the snow
which is saving itself for later: the snow in waiting.
A clock spreads out its hands. It is long ago.

In cold glass fronting the bookcase fires are burning:
soft russets, browns, fribbles of gold lace
flicker a glance from where bent backs are leaning
and print is a dry kiss on a yellowing face.

He can hear the pages fidget about and whisper,
stretch themselves out a little, breathe a sigh
through seas of ink and a mapped world of paper.
Christmas, nodding the sleepymen from his eye,

splits the warm light, nibbles away the evening,
waxed in thick scarlets, greens. The mistletoe
hangs in a chandelier of moony nothings;
a lost December is turning its lights down low

but the child reads on and on, till the house is floating
its gingerbread and its brick to words and signs
that the child has found before: the words in waiting.
The house is reading itself between his lines

to a nest of smells, a wrinkle of hands and voices,
the leafy twists and turns of a tangled maze:
it is three wishes, a hide-and-seek of faces,
a north of the north wind and a round of days

where fear, pressed like a leaf between his pages,
lurks in the bedroom and the droning sky;
curtains and walls go crumbly at the edges,
a dream is a dark lantern to steer him by.

He sleeps. The night babbles on in its cold coven
sunk deep in the wild wood where the wild things are;
somewhere the snow lies deep and crisp and even,
printed with neat runes. Somewhere there is a star

and a dark tree, scented, decked and tender,
the text of its leaves rubbed into vanishing:
an old house webbed in these words, and under,
the shade of a child who reads, a clock ticking.

Lawnheads Avenue

Down Lawnheads Avenue –
huge cold, huger stars –
the child who'll be a father,
the father once a child,
tip and tilt between them
a black and awkward tree

for Hansel, Gretel wish you
a Fröhliche Weinachten;
in Cologne's cathedral
the wolves of the schützstaffel
smile upon their children,
howl out their stille nacht.

Round the frozen corner
where the garden gate
snicks its snickersee,
the little shouldered tree
rises to the occasion,
takes aim at the moon

and all of us go dancing
into yellow hall-light,
holding hands and yawning
before the party frocks
catch upon the candles
and tishoo, all fall down.

It's a just-so story –
Something much like that.
I can see their shadows
crossed, but not for luck,
on balks and mounds of weather
curdled into snow.

Hurrel's Walk

Never knew how to spell it,
Hurrel's Walk, that swerve
of grey on sullen grey:
chewed hexagons of stone
packed out with dust and green,
a dull, undying sheen

where village women trudge
backed, faced, by eastern wind:
chapped lips, prams, mouse-hair –
paper-bagged, threadbare.
High nests go caw, caw,
and something red and raw

under it all – that house
shipwrecked and grey, its panes
floating black ripples over
its rifled honeycombs;
those gingerbread brick walls,
the greasy gleam of laurels.

At night, the restless air
drones of the dead, a woman
drowsed over book and glass
till print charred into flame:
the whole house simmering,
the rooks clamouring.

Her dream smokes into mine;
curtains filter the moon.
She wavers up and down,
a torch stuck in the wind
with her waxed, ancient look,
spelling her name on the dark

and the village falls away
into an echoing well
whose oily water shines
with timid ghosts of flame,
and elmed rooks make rook-talk:
'Hurrel's Walk, Hurrel's Walk'.

Green Boy

Did you look through the branches,
your gaze steady, till the summer-sweat
scalded and scaled your broken skin?
         Did your eyes

bring back a piece of jigsaw light,
cut like an oak leaf, holding a skull
to fit the bones that laced the ground
         when shot and shell

riddled the range to no great answer,
petrol cans asleep at their posts
nodded their heads in the rusting air?
         What do you see now?

The leaves are a tussle of green fingers;
I can see acorns, beech mast, soldiers
dancing with their own ghosts in half-light.
         I can hear laughter,

feel sharp-set wires twist to bramble;
the wood is ringed with spent violence
and a rabbit skull, delicate in grey,
         drops from my hand,

nuzzles down to its own scatterings,
and gathering sinew, fur and tendon
lopes off as a camouflaged truck, starting,
         whirrs at the hill's foot.

Reaches: 1946

for John Roddis

Never twice in the same water, but Hauxton's willows
still trail leaves over those rippled shadows thrown
by boys grown old, their feet still trapped in the shallows,
and a mill wheel which for years has forgotten to turn

its lazy buckets, jammed fast in our sweltering weather,
with other stuff that is going today for a song.
Under that parched roof dust-motes and mice gather
to consider machinery, which will not last long

as it rots into this endless, grand wateriness
dazed into darkness where our floats bob, rods lean,
bare legs tugged by a gentle, urgent wateriness –
as a mother tugs at a child in a crowded scene –

and small things – straws, burnt boats, are pulled to lodges
under the bridge, where echoes grow sybilline,
telling of water which flowed under other bridges
in halloos and catcalls which are yours, are mine,

as with doubled voices we follow the swift mill-leat
from where the green silks pour, though anchored, to where,
on its dazzled bed, a miller's thumb, spatulate,
rides on its shadow. The mill grinds the summer air

to invisible bread, and the bridge circles the summer
in half-moons of rich, cool water and molten blue;
echo on echo the years elide and shimmer,
pass themselves carelessly on, and under, and through.

Night Moles: Cambridge

I have been here before, and know
the sweet keen smell from the urinal's stalls,
the so-called gents bobbing it up and down.

We loitered by the railings, clock and cock
minatory and golden on the Catholic steeple
as orange and ostrich royalty waved by.

A scatter of black Austins made its stop and go,
and I lost half-a-crown and Churchill an election –
that smile on Peter Frampton's face in '45!

They buried the convenience at the crossroads.
I have a stake in its heart, that bolt-hole
from the Perse's stinking horse-troughs.

Not lost, but gone below: greenery, porcelain,
dirty iron, damp-souled cupboardings.
A night on the tiles for the famous Cambridge five,

swallowing each other's mirrored messages,
(Cyrillic script on Izal toilet paper),
planting devices behind unflushing cisterns,

while from the Polar Institute, the Leys,
ghosts eager for a pee dodge the new traffic,
cry to tarmac, *Leeve mooder, leet me in!*

(After all, this *is* Cambridge)

and a huge G.I. gives me a huge white grin,
brandishing his airship of an organ:
'Whaddaya think the girls want with it, sonny?'

Umbrella Man

Their smoky voices linger. Past the sill
it looks like rain again, it looks like rain:
wind at a soft-shoe shuffle, vaudeville
to set the flower-heads jigging off again.
Under these tilted clouds the out-of-doors
is follow-spots and ripples of applause.

Singling some seconds out from seventy years,
I watch an audience clap their hands away:
nice people with nice habits, ranked in tiers,
who watch their children trip in roundelay
and twirl the petal-pink of parasols –
O little eyases, neat dancing dolls!

They take each other's hands, then hold them out
to where the school roof makes its final bow:
players too young to know, too young to doubt
that they have hearts to break, or mend, who now,
as though the rocking future has not been,
re-trace the footsteps of an old routine

with Flanagan and Allen, strolling still
about their catchy tune that keeps off rain.
Whatever knives grow sharp, whatever will
go on its way and not come back again,
those dawdled voices wheedle us to keep
faith with what good boys pray for before sleep.

'Market Rasen Nostalgia'

Mr. J. Mendham appears to be setting up a Market Rasen record by having destroyed 45 wasps' nests this season. The Queen Wasps, happily quite dead, were brought to the Mail Office as evidence yesterday by Mr. F. Clark.

The Rasen Mail, *1940*

Mr. F. Clark wrinkles his face at the sun,
steadies a barrow full of smells and shade
where I lie low, tussling with a giant bear.
Something hopeless in the air, called Peace,
plucks at watch chains, flowers and waistcoats,
gets lost in shrubberies and terrier Jim,
tangled legless at the feet of Mr. J. Mendham,
who appears to be setting up as dog-in-the-manger.
A wing-beat of light trembles over the grass,
my grandfather's rolled sleeves, the gardener's coat,
splayed out, just held on the top button.
Mother's Kodak takes a Market Rasen record.

Mr. J. Mendham, now dug-in for victory,
brings down wrath on Rasen's paper tenements,
gummed-up ministries that snore with rumour,
till everyone, quite happily, is dead and dry.
Acts of gallantry need an officer witness,
a man whose medal, ribboned in red, white, black –
For faithful service in the Special Constabulary –
lies coffined in my father's cigarette-box.
So, each crusty sprig of suspect Royalty
is taken to the Mail for propaganda purposes.
Evidence? Those post-war aerial surveys:
each cell a cenotaph: life shrivelled to whisper.

Playtime in a Cold City

Emmanuel College, Cambridge. 1954–1957

... the last years of an exclusive masculine pastoral; snug studies, gas fires, lamplight, ghost-stories, fog at the windows. Cold staircases with bare light bulbs, fine rooms, sometimes stupendously fine rooms opening off them...
Peter Davidson, 'Secret Cambridge', from English Anxieties
by Tim Brennan (Photoworks, 2009)

*Remembering John Hadwen and Tony Glover
and for Desmond Gailey and Carola Scupham*

Prologue: Negative Space

No matter yesterday how clouds were backed.
Animal contours float over us for ever
whose stretched skins, belly-upward looks

breed definitions of lost space, lost time
contingent on those puzzling malformations:
tracts of sky-jungle for our philosophising.

It is the in-betweenness of it all,
the precise shape of each all-important absence
that takes the eye, that takes the eye away

into blue's fugitive laughter, the sighs of grey:
the fields of youth which hold those amities
forgotten words were found to certify,

words lost between the saying of leaves
chattering and whispering over running water,
hovering between new market conversations,

climbing a college stair, fidgeting up airily
against the downward drag, the clatter
and rush of new words tumbling down,

out into spaces between stone and stone
as white and filmy as a medium's gauze,
as a sky-creature at its brief touch-down.

Michaelmas Term, 1954

A box or two of books, an old cabin trunk
strapped on the rusty grid
of a 1930s Daimler fixed-head coupé –

a period piece run out of period.
A college landlady, granny-bosomed
with the milk of human kindness

cosying over a cosiness of ghosts,
brown furniture, an evensong
of elderly clergymen in college scarves.

Skins of light and cold.
After Grace, the brief nesting-pother
of male bottoms benching themselves

for feeding time: that low roar and growl
stared through by red and black divines
framed in twists of barley sugar.

Obligatory: the duffle coat from Millet's,
the provisional friends, the new pipe,
the first essay: The Fool's role in *Lear*.

A Gothic shell, alive with hermit crabs.
Held to the ear, such snarl and purr-miaow:
robes and furred gowns. The chew of cud,

the little bat-squeaks of dismantled poems
pleading softly to be re-assembled.
Surely we'd done this with our Bren guns?

Playtime in a Cold City

For children of fireweed, sirens, barrack squares,
pre-emptive strikes and midnight conversation,
it is playtime in a cold city. Three locust years.
We watch with incurious fascination

as clout upon trembling clout, this giant ball
brings Rance's Folly sliding to the ground;
banquet and roof-top tennis, fix-and-deal,
waft up and away to never-never land –

Victorian ghostlife, pushing fists of cloud
past lookalikes of chimneys, windows, doors.
The breeze swings on its hinge; a gaseous shroud
street-corners it about some sad-case stairs

and this dull thing clubbing the old stuff dead:
stahlhelm, the mailed fist in the mailed glove
at home with oak leaf, laurel, the nipped bud,
a new imperium come to push and shove

the fancy work, the possibly loved, the known
to shock-waves riding over a dirt floor.
Home-truths for us: the rubble, the skin-and-bone,
the cuff and growl, the stretch of the Bear's paw.

Father

He's been standing there some thirty years
in a crook of the chapel wall. Angular shade
sharpens its demand. His muscles

drive such easy, adequate gestures,
ripple carelessly under rumpled whites
trimmed with frippets of cerise and navy.

One of the cleverest undergraduates in my care,
athletic abilities of an unorthodox kind,
the real creative intelligence for two or three –

not all of this college – who cut a figure
in undergraduate literary circles of the day.
So his tutor, Welbourne, now Master.

Often I swing or dawdle through him,
squash racket in hand, prattling away
with a headful of friends and furious fancies,

past the plaque to the SONS OF THIS HOUSE,
the unlit blanks of stained-glass windows,
the pond patrolled by Swan and Edgar.

Emmanuel Athletes, 1924. No one smiles.
The neat faces of younger brothers,
hover between the trenches and the blitz,

all their steadied eyes caught in a Cyclops eye
by Stearn & Sons, Cambridge photographers.
Lions rampant dance over their hearts

and a second catches its breath, as he stares,
dark, intense, standing there in my light,
before their spring day fidgets itself into life,

takes its short run, then off, and into the dark.

The English Faculty, or Sweetness and Light

With acknowledgements to an article by J.B.P., 'The Early Installation of Electric Lighting in Emmanuel College', Emmanuel College Magazine, Lent Term, 1906

When my father was up, *entre deux guerres*,
and Quiller-Couch would saunter in from riding,
the stocked Gentleman of Letters, his quirt dangling,

it was one of those engines that can be hauled about,
with cylinder and crank set above the boiler.
The fitting was done in somewhat primitive fashion.

But the whole shebang needed practical criticism
from men prepared to get their hands dirty
up to the elbows in stock responses, ambiguity.

At a private view of the new light it was found
that the engine governor had been wrongly set –
a row of red-hot wires with intermittent darkness.

The present situation is of gas engines with boosters.
There are arrangements for silencing the exhaust,
which reaches air as a gentle puff through a pipe.

Mishaps include unequal pressure, hot bearings,
the discontent of the independent outward bearing,
the extreme discomfort of the big end.

Want of tightness has led to a continual jerking action,
the big end working loose from the crank,
the piston becoming a projectile.

Broken belting once missed the driver by inches,
there have been mishaps to the ignition tubes.
The governing is of the usual hit-and-miss type.

'I don't think we need bother with him,' says Dr Leavis,
holding up a minor Victorian by the tail
and dropping him on the lectern like a dead rat.

There are many things in gas-engine running
best learnt by experience.
Cylinder lubrication is all important.

So we go punting.

Long Vacation, August 1955

Army Emergency Reserve

'Arrived at the canvas mansions of the blest, seven a.m.
Rewarded for being nine hours early by nine hours duty
allocating fellaheen to their tents on complex little rotas.
The aristocracy? A research student in chemistry at King's
and a young whelp "getting his weight down for rugger".

Spent all night crawling about hills in driving rain –
since the enemy did not materialise, a friend and I
crawled forward and shot up our own troops with blanks.
Had not counted on retaliation – nearly blown to pieces
with thunderflashes – big Brock's Bangers.
The Teddy boys of the Lowlands screamed in wild euphony.
(The real attack didn't come till one in the morning.)

Have brought *Pater on the Renaissance,*
and, as always, *The London Book of English Verse.*

In this pantomime all the characters
are the wicked nephews of wicked uncles.
I am writing by a jar of misty moonbeams
escaping through the black glass of a stable lantern
subsisting on an apology for paraffin
in a damp, duckboarded tent in an acre of grass
in a well-known unbeauty spot close to nowhere.

Might just volunteer next year for further training –
probably with B.A.O.R. in Germany and the Herrenvolk!
The inducement? A stripe to bring me to sergeant.
Added emoluments would undoubtedly materialise.
Shall only bring about six pounds back to Cambridge.

This is the most bloody unhygienic place I've ever seen –
expect me home on a stretcher with typhoid.
The address is Annan Road Camp, A.E.R., Kirtlebridge,
near Lochabie (as in baby on the treetops), Dumfries.

Amendment: LOCKERBIE.'

'God with us'

In the howse of pure Emanuel
I had my Education;
Where my friends surmise
I dazeld mine Eyes
With the Light of Revelation...

                                    Richard Corbett

Our college stones are pitted by controversy
patrolled by Black Friars, puritans, platonists –
gowns flagged out by acidulous eastern winds.

At Great St Mary's the egregious Stockwood
mourns the Church's death; files his congregation
past a coffin – empty, but for a mirror,

and the Cambridge Inter-Collegiate Christian Union,
still high on memories of Billy Graham,
prowls earnestly for our unavailable souls.

Dear John, whose missionary father
survived Changi to die on an English beach,
lives in his absence, compounding grief and guilt –

Jutty with justice, grey like a prison,
Across the ball-tossing line leaving the sea
He ran dead at my feet –

while night after night we keep sharp vigil.
Shall we smoke God out of his non-existence,
armed with Lewis's insidious comminations,

inklings from Sayers and Charles Williams?
For now, let Bach and Hopkins annotate
the plain texts of our noncomformity.

In this dark January, the Dean of Kings
plunges to his death from Lawrence's 'upturned sow'
styed in those mannerly, sardonic precincts,

and I write to Oxford: 'Remember, Ramsay was a Scot.
To hurl oneself off one's chapel roof in a gale
was considered here a wild Stuart thing to do.'

Cambridge dances hand-in-hand with darkness,
darkness and cold. Pressing into desolation,
each Wehrmacht soldier's buckle bore the motto –

Gott mit uns.

Mind Games

As for the party, we enjoyed ourselves.
Tony and I constituted ourselves spokesmen
of Hub College, to which great institution
we drank innumerable toasts. I, in my new role
as a visiting oceanographer from Seattle,
told a furious Neil his new seahorseshoes
had not been properly nailed on.

We measured space in different directions,
finding it decreased in proportion
as to the less it was measured. With difficulty
we kept it static by allowing it two minutes' rest
between our scientific interferences.

Hypnotism is all the thing.
Dangerous, because he believes in ghosts
says Neil. I can't see the connection.

Stage set. Mind games. Swinging lights.
Counting. Regressing. Our willing pathic
balances his board-stiff body between chairs,
We are the connoisseurs of his indignity.
He ambles the room, looks for what isn't there.
Lost between the power-freaks and the suspicious,
we take him back, back to his London childhood –

Ghosts tower in a whirlwind of sobs and anger.
The raw, rough ghosts of love, and war, and pain
jostle in the shocked air between us,
deny measurement, deny proportion.

The lost faces, the cowering furniture –
half in tears as I write and think of it.

In the Dark

To John's rooms, mine, a shared set,
our friends clatter upstairs nightly:
Tony, drunk on Socratic interrogation,
Des, mathematician, embryo polymath.
Scholarship boys, off-the-leash puritans,
the clever, eager sons of widowed mothers.

John, ex-navigator, haunted
by a night flight nearly brought to grief
in a whirl of Yeatsian gyres and lunar phases,
mazed again as Tony, gunnery officer,
fires ranging shots at him from Wittgenstein.
Des, two years younger, fresh from Armagh,

studies, amused, our tribal customs.
Small hours grow thick with language;
the gas flusters away its long, soft snake-hiss.
Drunk on Nescafé and buttered sausages,
we hunt each other down like lost lovers
caught in a midwinter night's dream,

nailing ideas to the walls in shabby space.
watching them beat their heads on windows
rattling to a spatter-dash of wind and rain.
In Front Court, the chapel clock's
left, right, left, right paces a dead march
through road tunnel and monastic cloister,

past names that once defined our stair,
their white on black as painted out
as they themselves, as all our certainties.
We borrow more night, joust in shadows,
Tectonic plates grind and stir. In Moscow
Burgess and Maclean surface like dying goldfish.

Considerations

6 March 1956

My prospective father-in-law sits in his study
surrounded by yellowing copies of *The Times*,
Nigerian cloths, Peruvian pots, a shifting tidewrack
of academe. His cherry will soon come into flower.
He is considering me, considering his daughter
now reading Greats at Lady Margaret Hall.
'I appreciate your writing to ask for my consent.
Parents are not always consulted nowadays.
Of course, my answer is "in the affirmative".
I suppose you would not wish to contemplate marriage
until you have finished your exams, got a post
which will enable you to be independent...'

Our old headmaster, the Reverend P.M.S. Gedge,
one of that trio of Cambridge friends so wittily known
by rugger-buggers as 'The Three Must-get-beers',
and famous for his address on the Resurrection
which ponders the reunion of shaved-off facial hairs,
is considering me, my prospective father-in-law,
my father-in-law's daughter. Possibly my father,
a school governor. He switches to automatic pilot:
'With their brains, interests and common schooling...
A well-matched pair... A Marriage Guidance Course...
Should be aware of the ideals, trials and joys
of Christian Marriage... If the school premises...'

The marriage takes place a year later; the local rag
treads carefully on our unfamiliar eggshells:
The bride's father is the retired British Museum.
The bride-keeper of Ethnography at the groom's father
is the Director of Educational Services at the B.B.C.

In the Cold War you have to keep them guessing –
we write our essays on rice-paper, then eat them.

Notes from Oxford

Sir Maurice Bowra has been visiting the menagerie
and we were made to go through our tricks.
I was immune to the atmosphere of worldly well-being.

Professor Fraenkel he gave me (whoops! floating participle)
two and a half hours tutorial. Elegant and genteel,
not so much in appearance as in manners.
He is very sympathetic with young ladies
without the advantage of a public-school education –
but, of course, he has his ego to preserve.
Most of the time was spent in reading out Greek metre;
at one point he gagged me firmly with a piece of chocolate.
Like Clytemnestra and champagne, his words
are temporarily potent, but not lasting.

Went to Lord David Cecil on 'Biography'.
Had wanted to do one of Jane, but (with tears in his eyes)
Cassandra burnt all her love-letters, so no-go.

A very bad essay, finished at 2.10 this morning.
Took at least an hour over every sentence.
Paced round, played piano, wanted to come home
and have a nervous breakdown. Bee saved me.
Her pen begins to flow at about 3 a.m.,
so we played a duet and mourned over our symptoms.

Sound of mowing in distance, cricket-clapping –
all set for entry of Edwardian picnic;
I absorb the antique wisdom of Athenian philosophy –
'Philosophy is odious and obscure.'

Oxford – too much of it.

Loving wishes to all, Carola

What are we doing in this windy city,
John and I? Too old for this, at twenty-three,
gowns flapping in curtailed evening air.
John's in love; I am engaged to my Oxford girl.
Toytown. The Parade of the Tin Soldiers.

Mr Inventor, my friend Rodney,
ex Ed. Corps sergeant, gives up on Queens'
to marry Judith, pale and beautiful.

Queenie and F.R., experts in decontamination,
heat our library books in their furious ovens
to kill the bacilli of pleasure and endurance
that made our beds and barracks tolerable –
Mr and Mrs Growser, ruling and dividing.
Sly, I ask Leavis in a public lecture
what he thinks of Tolkien. 'Haven't read him.
Friends tell me he just can't do it, can't do it.'

Tom Henn, ex-Brigadier, unleashes Yeats:
'He shook me to tears. Only Henn can do it.'
The urbane Lucas says that most of us
think like pedants and write like grocers.

To King's for tutorials. Pip Gaskell, bibliographer,
played clarinet with Bechet, Lyttelton;
created the Reverend Theodore Snord
whose minor verse diddled the examiners.
He whisks us round King's portrait gallery.
'And this,' eyes twinkling, coat-tails flapping,
pointing to a large contemporary divine, 'is a portrait
of the most notorious sodomite in Cambridge.'
We gaze with due veneration.

Outside, by the Victorian pillar box,
Larry the Lamb – *I do my little be-e-est* –
clutches his lecture-notes. Dennis the Dachshund
cycles by in games-kit, balls hung low.

'My essays are funnier than ever.
I choose my own subject. Gaskell says hopefully
"And was he a poet this week, Peter?"
A twisted smile. Reading English is bloody silly,
As for finals, I shall rely on native wit
and my acknowledged grace of style,
I shall put down everything I can think of,
and praise all the authors I select,
that is assuming I can think of any authors.'

'The master expects you to do very well.
Are you going to get a First?'

No.

'They're Off!'

Part I, English Tripos, 1956

Mortar-boards in the air for foals and fillies:
It's a re-run of the 1956 Grand National.

Must is the favourite. (Sired by *Ought* out of *Don't*:
those well-groomed coursers from parental stables.)

Early Mist, a previous winner, is always a safe bet
here in Cambridge. (By *Cough* out of *Fog*.)

We jump *The Chair* of Medieval and Renaissance Studies,
stewarded by C.S. Lewis on *Perelandra* –

such power, such confidence. Bright Newnham babes
and John crouch loose-reined for their starred Firsts,

but some of us, who know better (or no better)
take our cue from dear old *Devon Loch*,

leap high in the air on the home straight,
pancake on our stomachs, keep buggering on,

trailed by also-rans, who, spooked by *Scrutiny*,
jump imaginary fences, cramp their hindquarters

through lecturettes, get nobbled by tight-arsed critics –
but, of course, we all win, and all have prizes.

As the Queen Mum and our tutors say:
'Oh, that's racing!'

Amours de Voyage

Summer, and here at the Mill, Lyttelton's playing, or Barber,
(*ac tuba terribili sonitu taratantara dixit*),
shaking the air to a music as throaty, sweet and as pungent
as a pint of Merrydown cider. An afternoon on the river,
three of us lolled on the cushions, one of us sliding the punt-pole,
tiring the sun with our talk, writing our names on the water:
Tony, his head in the clouds, unfolds the Investiture Contest,
Desmond preaches to ducks: his text the aesthetics of number,
John smiles, trailing his fingers, lost in that maze of reflection
which follows our slide into nowhere, while I, the tame dilettante,
boast of my find at the bookstall: a nice duodecimo Prior
with little bar-borders, vignettes, and in its original binding.
Yes, we are deeply in love: with ourselves, our verbal confections
which juggle, flicker and die as light hunts shade through the willows
and crew entangles with crew, and laughter entangles with laughter.

Somewhere away in the desert the might of infuriate Egypt
moves, with Slovakian arms, to sweep a nation to glory,
but our strong man, Anthony Eden (allow for the variant pronouns),
Dreamt of great indignations and angers transcendental,
Dreamt of a sword at his side and a battle-horse underneath him.
Nasser, take the Canal! Shall the lights dim out over Europe?
Shall punts meander no longer in safety through Grantchester
                                                    meadows?
Comes the man, cometh the hour. *Arma virumque canimus.*

Long Vacation, August 1956

Mobilisation of the Army Emergency Reserve

Brown envelope at nine. Battledress pressed and ironed
in a flurried kitchen. Be somewhere by 4.30.
The *Brief Encounter* bit. Whistle, clank and smuts.

Blackdown? Deepcut, waiting to become notorious?
The warrant has been made out incorrectly;
'Brookwood' is army-speak for 'Basingstoke'.

South of the border, down Aldershot way,
no one knows what's what or where is where,
certainly not what for, or for how long.

The station is deserted. No platform porters.
Just little me going off, or on. I lose myself
in miles of dusky huts, white cement kerbstones.

The notices grow minatory, indecipherable:
Nosmo King. Halt. Careless Talk Costs Wives.
I stumble on a guardroom, afloat in darkness,

am given blankets, told where I can sleep.
By eleven next morning I haven't found my Unit.
A Regular tells me soldiers have been seen

in a kind of dream-life, lying on beds,
laughing, being posted. Miraged houris
hover with camels, over Hampshire sand.

He guesses at six months. 'I might have rung you
but couldn't find the one and sixpence.
I'll tell you later if we ever get there.'

Get Well Soon

So corporal punishment has overtaken you –
and I signed the petition like anything, as well.
Are you yet a serjeant-at-arms, alone and palely loitering?
(For *La Belle Dame sans Merci* read Elizabeth R.)
You say you may go to the Middle East –
do you know anything about sandblasting?
John says it's amazing how heavy a haversack gets
if you try folding a mosquito net into it.
We wrote, as we said, a card to Carola,
born, if not of despair, at least of deep concern,
and invited her round to lunch in P4 on October 10th.
May your boots never fail to shine, your mien
never fail to impress the C.O. and the men.
May your buckles never lack polish, nor your trousers
a crease of outstanding rectilinearity,
nor your Naafi Cakes be dry, nor your tea gut-rotting.

The whole thing, of course, is damn nonsense –
the initial letters of your camp cannot be a coincidence.
I hope to goodness this thing does not come to pass –
je serais désolé.

Weather mild and considerate, like most of the natives;
we have a slate-roofed room here in a derelict cottage –
hay for our beds, torn from the farmer's ricks,
a tap outside the door, fresh butter, milk and eggs.
When we run out of wood, we tear some from the walls.
If you find the answers to this, or anything else,
Poste Restante, Armagh, will reach the better part of us.

What other best wishes are there?
Such as they are, let them rest between the lines.

Regards, Tony. See you soon, John.

A Somewhere Hut

Base Ammunition Depot, Cooper's Lane Camp, Bramley, Basingstoke.

'Rumours, drill, weapon-training, vaccination and medicals.
Your Hardy is getting to look a bit scuffed-up already.
No one seems to have done anything yet but laugh.
I can't find a telephone. There is tropical kit stored here.
Paint-blisters, bottles, cups and saucers have no significance.
There are huts somewhere, damp grass everywhere.'

Goon Show hilarity. All Chiefs, no Indians.
Gung-ho officers have no significance.
We paint big metal objects desert-yellow,
press Button A and ring home with new rumours,
lounge about with bottles, cups and saucers
while Hampshire roads go choc-a-bloc with armour.

My friend in the Atomic Energy Commission
puts my mind through drill and weapon-training;
we puzzle away at C.P. Snow's two cultures.
There's nothing like his mental vaccination
to laugh the rumours out of significance
in a somewhere hut stuck in a damp-grass nowhere,

where poor Tom Hardy's rain-soaked love-life
seems bleary as the sad-eyed Quartermaster.
Rumours as big as cats must all be signed for,
issued with mess-tins, sent for medicals,
marched, counter-marched and dosed with blisters,
scuffed up for weekend passes, foreign postings,

kitted most tropically for *fishing in the dull canal*
on a winter evening. Sitting on scuffed-up grass,
the Sergeant and I, Bramley's High Culture,
drill and polish an armoury of quotations;
rumours of time and circumstance go idling
past us. There is laughter, of no significance.

Back at dusk from my third embarkation leave
the Guard Commander grins – 'You jammy fucker.
The Duty Officer's got a War House telex:
If this reservist is still here in England
send him back immediately to Cambridge.
If abroad, you need take no further action.'

The Lady's Not For Burning

The Old Library, February, 1957

So, back again in this fretwork city
where crocket and finial scour the wind
and in westering sunlight a cold chapel,
manned by a stray organ-scholar,
throbs softly to bombarde and ophicleide

we sprawl on cushions, high on poetry
and the spindrift float of Palestrina, Monteverdi,
play 'Quotations', a pack of jokers
who take each other's tricks, chase time away
in a fug of smoke and laughter.

Drunk on Mr Polly's sesquippledan verboojuice,
cobwebbing the room's high corners
with Steerpike and Abiatha Swelter,
bewitched by Jennet and her Thomas Mendip,
what should we do, who live by fancy talk,

but set Fry's tuppenny-coloured puppets
off again? Tony and I gather our friends
 – *Perfectly young, obstreperously golden* –
rehearse flim-flam while Cold War glaciers
grow even colder, and the wolves start running.

A close-packed letter from Sergeant Cawley
briefs me on the ceasefire joys I missed:
a flight out in battered wartime Shackletons,
grovelling and guarding in the sand and dust
then home for Christmas on the carrier *Theseus*:

'a saga of heroism, glory and time wasted.
I hope you are well and happy. Preserve your star.
Norman.' This dark February we paint flats,
shuffle about in cable-stitch sweaters,
watch our scratch-cast pirouette on word-strings.

'Scene: the small market-town of Cool Clary',
(more commonly known to us as 'Cambridge'):
Here is such a storm of superstition
And humbug and curious passions, where will you start
To look for the truth?

Lost Hearts

A flutter at the gate, a dead knock in the wainscot,
a Chinese grandmother in the priest's oratory
a little book of appearances, disappearances –
    Shall we make *an evening's entertainment?*

'Not feeling so well at ease tonight – blue and rainy.
We all seem to be suffering from tedium vitae,
and go about with Saurian eyes, disconsolate mouths.'
    Are we *a warning to the curious?*

Shall we be dead to each other? Whose images
play with our unborn children in far fields,
walk neutral corridors, lit, but of no importance,
    prune dead thoughts in *the rose garden?*

'John feels his inaction is purposeless
We curse this Babylon which once was Mecca:
the realised promise of the enchanted isles.'
    How long shall we sit here, *casting the runes*

while porters chunter over their skeleton keys,
and I read aloud to my sprawled friends from Owen:
I am the ghost of Shadwell Stair... Mist-shrouds
    draw over and about *the haunted dolls' house,*

this restless lumber of echoes, bells, faces,
square courts packed with circular argument
where the future whispers to each its blandishment:
    Oh, whistle, and I'll come to you, my lad.

Unfoldings

In this last May's
warm unfoldings of sweet air,
barely sleeping, we sleep bare
and slip dew

to the Fellows' Garden,
a cool spring water
sacred to the Muses.
Shake the glass

and flesh sparkles.
Quick voices, far, far, far.
John's nonchalant dive
splinters daylight

and we are baptised,
confirmed in fellowship
by ungowned signs, tokens
of meshed life

green and quickening,
careless of degree and custom
as the lit faces of dead friends,
laughing.

Epilogue: Whatever Happened?

Whatever happened never happened next.
Forget the rags, the riches, glittering prizes:
just young men kicking up each other's heels

in their masculine pastoral, where the nymphs
cycle to morning lectures, arrange wide skirts
as punts from Scudamore's idle through the Backs,

go to May Balls where Tommy Kinsman plays
selections from *The Boy Friend, Salad Days* –
our rifles have not yet turned into guitars,

nor we into our past: no Aegean cruises,
no candled dish of flummery at High Table,
our Augean stables cleansed for a quick sleep-over,

no doormat brochures of nice boys and girls
playing with processors in study bedrooms,
cooing enchantments to the middle-aged.

Duffle coats and winter mists set in,
the drowned boys hover over Byron's Pool,
loneliness dies, huddled by his unlit gas,

and Elvis shakes away 'Heartbreak Hotel'.
Squirrels and Bears eat each other's hearts out;
Soviet tanks grind into Budapest.

Eskimo Toys

Life, journeys, a sledge roped with trophies,
the blank sound of a howling wilderness,
shawls, wet pelts, fur, scales of skin –
the blue cold carves these things down to the bone,

maps them. Bare things bare again to crystal,
poetry, the pure hexameters of snow.
Eyes glitter more brightly for the dark,
the stars unsheathed, their lights far and northern.